Cat Crafts

Written and Illustrated by
Linda Hendry

KIDS CAN PRESS

For Errol and Finn

Text and illustrations © 2002 Linda Hendry

KIDS CAN DO IT and the logo are trademarks of Kids Can Press Ltd.

Kids Can Press acknowledges the support of the Government of Canada, through the BPIDP, for our publishing activity.

Published in Canada by
Kids Can Press Ltd.
29 Birch Avenue
Toronto, ON M4V 1E2

Published in the U.S. by
Kids Can Press Ltd.
2250 Military Road
Tonawanda, NY 14150

www.kidscanpress.com

Edited by Laurie Wark
Designed by Karen Powers
Photography by Frank Baldassarra
Printed in Hong Kong by Wing King Tong Company Limited

The hardcover edition of this book is smyth sewn casebound.
The paperback edition of this book is limp sewn with a drawn-on cover.

CM 02 0 9 8 7 6 5 4 3 2 1
CM PA 02 0 9 8 7 6 5 4 3 2 1

National Library of Canada Cataloguing in Publication Data

Hendry, Linda
Cat crafts

(Kids can do it)

Includes index.

ISBN 1-55074-964-1 (bound)   ISBN 1-55074-921-8 (pbk.)

1. Handicraft — Juvenile literature. 2. Cats — Juvenile literature. I. Title. II. Series.

SF447.3.H44 2002   j745.5   C2001-900827-9

Kids Can Press is a Nelvana company

Contents

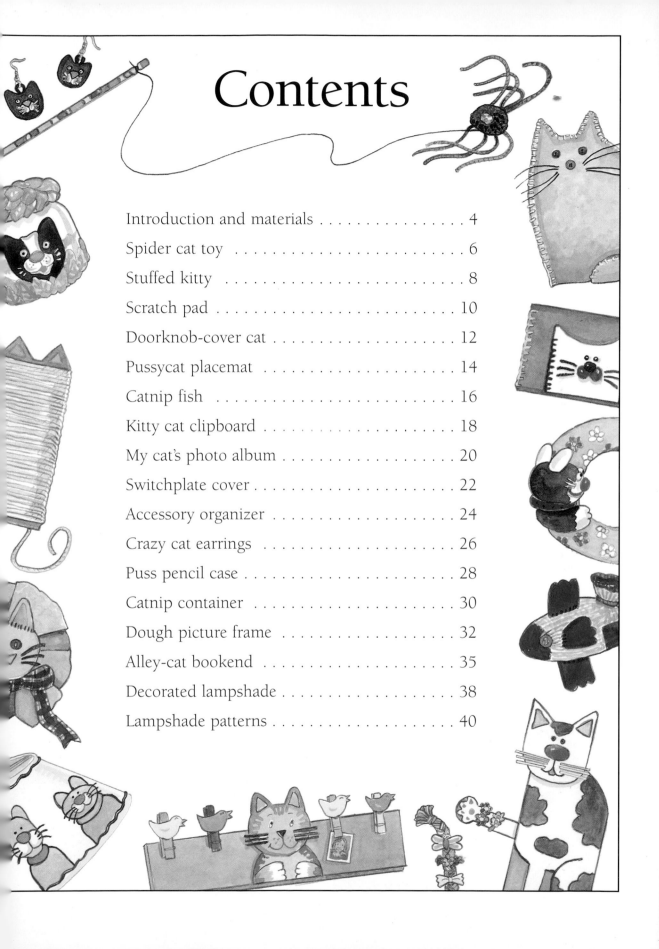

Introduction

This book is chock-full of craft ideas that make a PURRRfect gift for a cat lover — or a cat! Learn how to make a kitty clipboard or alley-cat bookends for your room, a photo album or picture frame for your aunt, crazy cat earrings for your sister and even a catnip fish for a furry friend!

MATERIALS

These crafts are made from easy-to-find materials. Many supplies can be found around your home. A craft supply store should have the materials you need to buy. Before you begin, cover your work surface with newspaper to protect it from glue and paint.

Cardboard

Some projects require corrugated cardboard or light cardboard. Corrugated cardboard is used to make boxes for heavy things. Ask your grocer for a box. Crackers and cereal come in boxes made from light cardboard.

Glue

White, non-toxic glue is strong and dries clear. Have a few clothespins on hand when you are gluing. They can often be used to hold pieces together while they dry.

Scissors and utility knives

You can do most of the cutting in this book with a pair of sharp scissors. If you are cutting cardboard or paper and would like a straighter edge, use a utility knife and a metal-edged ruler. Always ask an adult to help you use a utility knife, and protect your working surface with a piece of corrugated cardboard.

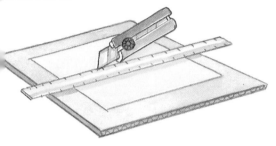

Paints and paintbrushes

Acrylic craft paints come in lots of colors, and they give your project a smooth finish. They dry quickly, so place only as much as you need onto a piece of wax paper.

Use a small pointed brush for painting details. Flat straight-edged brushes can be used for painting larger areas. Clean your brushes with water before changing color and rinse them well when you are finished painting.

Sewing

To make the Stuffed Kitty on page 8 and the Puss Pencil Case on page 28, you must know how to do a blanket stitch. Follow the diagrams below.

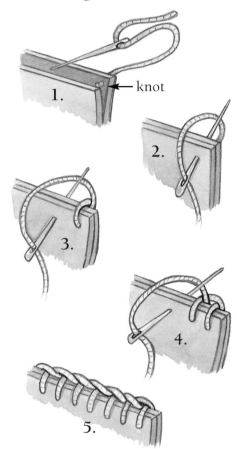

Measuring

Measurements are given in both metric and imperial. Choose one measurement system and use it for the entire project.

Safety note

Remember to check your cat's toys regularly to make sure there are no loose bits or pieces that could harm your pet.

Spider cat toy

Use this cat toy like a fishing rod. With a jingling spider for bait, you're sure to catch yourself a nice big furry "catfish."

YOU WILL NEED

- a piece of 1 cm (½ in.) dowel about 66 cm (26 in.) long
- black or navy blue yarn
- a piece of string about 86 cm (34 in.) long
- a small craft jingle bell
- a utility knife, paint, a paintbrush, scissors

1 Ask an adult to cut a notch near one end of the dowel as shown. Paint the dowel and set it aside to dry.

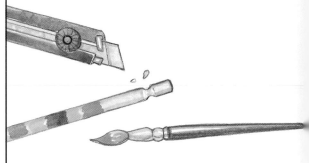

2 Cut four 30 cm (12 in.) pieces of yarn and set them aside. These will be the spider's legs.

3 To make a pom-pom for the spider's body, hold three fingers o[f] one hand slightly apart and loosely win[d] about 60 loops of yarn around them.

4 Hold the pieces of yarn from step 2 together and wrap them around the loops of yarn and tie a loose knot.

7 Cut the loops open, trim the pom-pom, and fluff it up. Do not trim the legs.

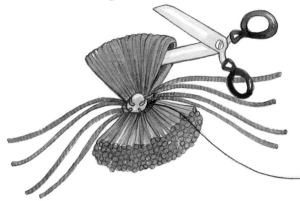

5 Gently slide the loops off your fingers and pull the knot tight in the center of the loops. Tie a triple knot. You now have eight spider legs.

8 To tie the spider to the dowel, wrap the string tightly around the notch two or three times and knot it.

6 Wrap one end of the string around the middle of the loops. Slide the bell onto the string and tie a tight triple knot to hold it in place.

Stuffed kitty

Your bed would make a good home for this cozy cat pillow. Or give it to a friend who doesn't have a pet.

YOU WILL NEED

- a piece of paper 45 cm x 28 cm (18 in. x 11 in.)
- a piece of fuzzy felt or fleece 45 cm x 56 cm (18 in. x 22 in.)
- 3 buttons, 2 black and 1 pink
- black and pink thread
- embroidery floss or yarn and a darning needle
- fiberfill stuffing
- a pencil, straight pins, scissors, a needle, masking tape

1 On the paper, draw the cat shape as shown and cut it out to make a pattern.

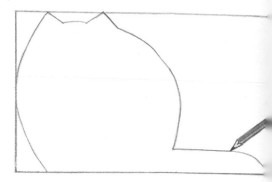

2 Place the felt right side down and fold the short sides together. Place the pattern along the fold and pin it in place through both layers of felt. Cut out the cat shape. **Do not cut along the fold.** Remove the pins and pattern.

3 On one half of the cat, sew on the buttons for eyes and a nose.

4 For whiskers, cut a piece of black thread 55 cm (22 in.) long. Thread it onto the needle and pull the ends even. Push the needle through the felt and back again, leaving a loop the back. Tie a knot in the loop, pull the whiskers tight, and tape the loop to the felt. Repeat on the other side.

5 Cut the thread to remove the needle, then repeat step 4 with other piece of thread on the other le of the nose and trim the whiskers.

6 Thread the darning needle with embroidery floss and blanket stitch (see page 5) around the tail.

7 Stuff the tail with fiberfill. Use a pencil to push the stuffing to the end.

8 Continue blanket stitching until you have a 10 cm (4 in.) opening. Stuff the pillow until it is firm, then blanket stitch the opening.

Scratch pad

To attract your cat to its new scratching pad, try rubbing the twine with a bit of catnip.

YOU WILL NEED

- 2 pieces of corrugated cardboard, each 13 cm x 33 cm (5 in. x 13 in.)
- a ball of twine
- scissors, a pencil, white glue, masking tape, a craft stick
- paint and a paintbrush (optional)

1 Cut two triangle-shaped ears at the top of one piece of cardboard. Place it on the other piece and trace around the ears. Cut out the shape and glue the two pieces together. Let them dry.

2 To make a loop for hanging, cut a 45 cm (18 in.) piece of twine and tie a double knot at each end. Form a loop and tape it to the cardboard as shown.

3 To make the tail, cut a 50 cm (20 in.) piece of twine, tie a double knot at one end, and tape it to the bottom corner of the cardboard.

5 Continue applying glue and wrapping the twine in small sections until the cat's entire body is covered.

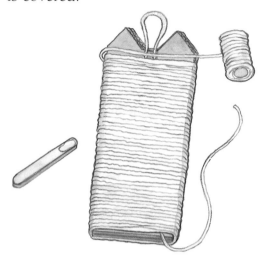

4 Starting at the bottom, spread glue on a small section of the front and back of the cardboard with the craft stick. Place the end of the twine in one corner as shown and wrap the twine tightly around the cardboard.

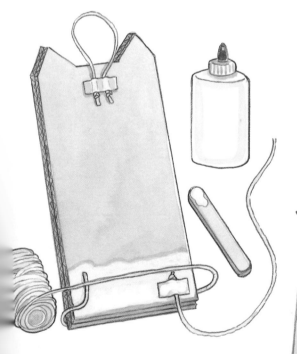

6 Trim the twine and let the scratch pad dry completely. If you like, paint a pink triangle in the middle of each ear.

7 Hang the scratch pad on a doorknob and call your kitty.

Doorknob-
cover cat

*This brave kitty cover will protect your
wall from doorknob dents.*

YOU WILL NEED

- a piece of gray felt
23 cm x 23 cm (9 in. x 9 in.)
- a piece of fiberfill quilt batting
18 cm x 18 cm (7 in. x 7 in.)
- scraps of pink felt
- 2 buttons
- a piece of black yarn 30 cm (12 in.) long
and a darning needle
- a piece of ribbon 86 cm (34 in.) long
- scissors, white glue, a needle and thread

1 Fold the gray felt in half, and then
in half again. Cut the corner as
shown. Unfold the felt. You should
have a circle.

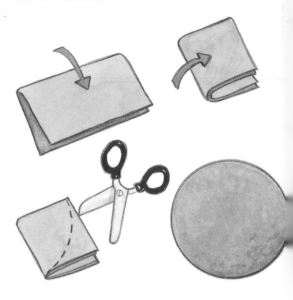

2 Fold and cut the quilt batting as
you did in step 1 to make a circle.
Glue the batting to the felt. Let the
glue dry.

3 To make a nose, cut a small triangle of pink felt and glue it to the center of the felt circle.

4 Sew the buttons on for eyes.

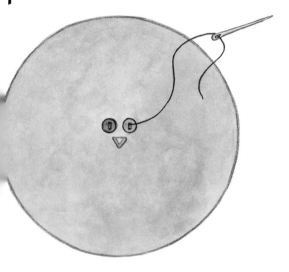

5 Cut two triangle-shaped ears from scraps of gray felt. Cut two slightly smaller pink triangles and glue one onto each gray triangle. When they are dry, sew the ears onto the circle of felt.

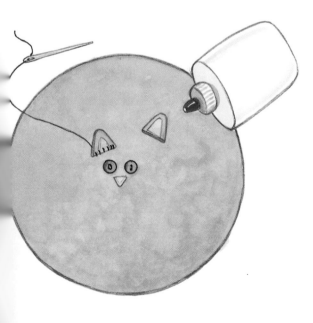

6 For whiskers, thread the yarn onto the darning needle and knot one end. Pull the yarn through the batting and felt until the knot is snug. Trim the yarn, leaving a 2.5 cm (1 in.) whisker. Tie another knot in the yarn and pull it through to make another whisker. Make more whiskers, then apply glue to each knot to hold the whiskers in place. Let the glue dry.

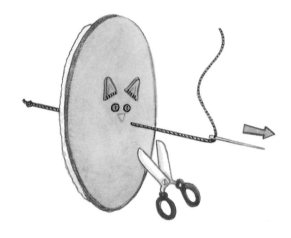

7 Center the cover on your doorknob and push back the sides. Wrap the ribbon tightly around the cover and tie it securely. Finish by tying a bow.

Pussycat placemat

This vinyl-covered placemat makes cleaning up after a messy eater a breeze.

YOU WILL NEED

- a piece of newsprint
  30 cm x 40 cm (12 in. x 16 in.)
- a piece of bristol board
  30 cm x 40 cm (12 in. x 16 in.)
- photocopies or magazine pictures of cats
- colorful stickers or shapes
  cut from paper (optional)
- 2 sheets of clear, self-adhesive vinyl,
  each 35 cm x 45 cm (14 in. x 18 in.)
- a pencil, scissors, a glue stick

1 Fold the newsprint in half, long sides together, and draw half of a fish shape as shown. Cut it out to make a pattern.

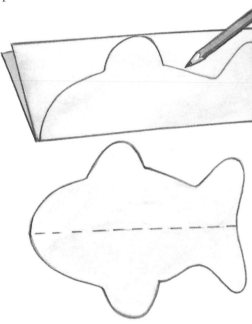

2 Unfold the pattern and trace it onto the bristol board. Cut out the placemat.

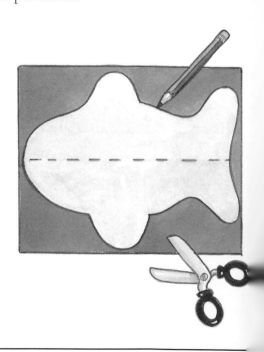

3 Put the cat pictures on the placemat. When you like the design, glue the pictures in place. Trim any that stick over the edge.

4 If you like, add stickers or paper shapes to your design.

5 Peel the backing paper off one sheet of vinyl. With the picture side down, center the placemat on the sticky side of the vinyl. Press firmly and smooth out the placemat.

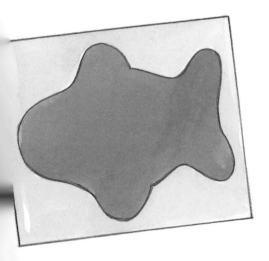

6 Peel back one long edge of the other sheet of vinyl and carefully line it up with one long edge of the first piece. Smooth out the vinyl and peel away a bit more of the backing. Continue to smooth the vinyl and remove the backing until the entire sheet is in place.

7 Turn the placemat over. Smooth out any wrinkles or bubbles, then trim the placemat, leaving a small margin of vinyl around the edges.

Catnip fish

Ever wonder what to do with all those socks that have no mates? Why not make a sockeye salmon for your cat to play with?

YOU WILL NEED

- fiberfill stuffing
- dried catnip
- a sock
- yarn and a darning needle
- scraps of felt
- 2 small buttons
- scissors

1 Mix a pinch of catnip into the stuffing, and stuff the sock until it's plump right up to the ankle.

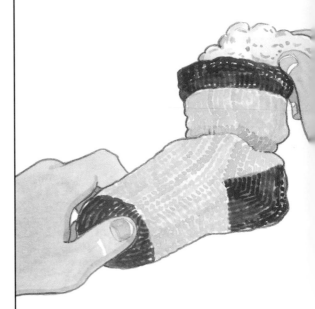

2 Cut a piece of yarn 20 cm (8 in.) long and wrap it tightly around the ankle of the sock. Tie a double knot and trim the ends.

3　Cut two small fins from felt and sew them to the sides with the yarn.

5　Tie a triple knot in the end of the yarn and push the needle through near the toe of the sock. Thread one button onto the needle and yarn. Push the needle back through the button and through to the other side of the sock.

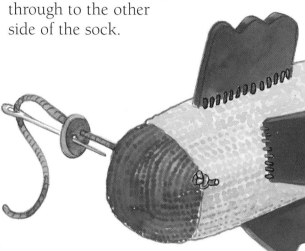

4　Cut two slightly larger fins and sew them to the top and bottom the fish.

6　Thread the second button onto the needle and continue to sew the buttons onto the sock by passing the needle back and forth through both buttons. Pull the yarn snug to create an indent around each eye. To finish, tie a triple knot close to one button and trim the ends.

17

Kitty cat clipboard

This cool cat can help you organize your room. Or use it in the kitchen to pin up lists.

YOU WILL NEED

- corrugated cardboard,
1 piece 10 cm x 45 cm (4 in. x 18 in.),
1 piece 10 cm x 15 cm (4 in. x 6 in.),
4 pieces each 4 cm x 5 cm (1½ in. x 2 in.)

- 6 pieces of dry spaghetti,
each 5 cm (2 in.) long

- 4 wooden clothespins, painted

- paints, paintbrushes, a pencil, scissors,
white glue, a hammer and 2 small nails

1 Paint the long strip of cardboard green and set it aside to dry.

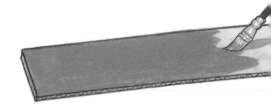

2 Following the steps below, draw the cat shape on the 10 cm x 15 cm (4 in. x 6 in.) piece of cardboard.

3 Cut out the cat shape and paint it. Set it aside to dry.

6 Glue the cat to the center of the green strip. Glue two clothespins on each side of the cat as shown. When they are dry, glue a bird near the top of each clothespin.

7 To hang your clipboard, ask an adult to hammer a nail through each end of the green strip.

4 Paint the pieces of spaghetti. Let them dry, then glue them in to make whiskers.

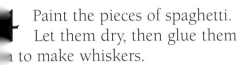

5 Draw a bird shape on each of the four small pieces of cardboard. Cut them out and paint them. Set them aside to dry.

My cat's photo album

Show off your cat photos in this kitty-shaped album. If you have a lot of photos, make a few extra pages.

YOU WILL NEED

- bristol board, 6 black pieces each 14 cm x 20 cm (5 1/2 in. x 8 in.), 2 yellow pieces each 18 cm x 22 cm (7 in. x 8 1/2 in.)
- 2 pieces of yarn or string, each 30 cm (12 in.) long
- a pencil, scissors, a hole punch, masking tape, a ruler, a table knife, markers or crayons
- self-adhesive photo corners or tape

1 Place one piece of black bristol board on top of one piece of yellow, lining up the bottoms. Draw the cat shape on the yellow piece as shown. Set the black piece aside and cut out the shape.

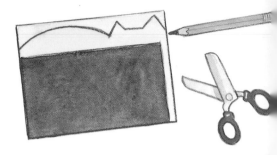

2 Trace the cat shape onto the second piece of yellow bristol board and cut it out. These are the covers.

3 On one piece of black bristol board, punch five evenly spaced holes along one short side. Using this as a pattern, trace the holes onto the remaining pieces of black bristol board and punch them out. These are the pages.

4 Place one page on a cover with the holes at the tail end of the cat shape as shown. Trace the holes and punch them out. Repeat this for the second cover.

6 Lay the ruler beside the holes on the front cover, and run the table knife along the ruler. Open the cover along the line.

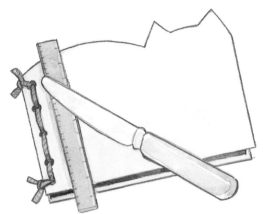

5 Wrap one end of each piece of yarn with a small piece of tape (this will make it easier to sew with). Place the pages between the covers and align the holes. Stitch the album together as shown. Tie the ends of the yarn with a double knot. Trim.

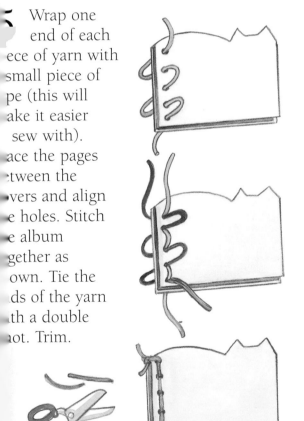

7 Color the front and back covers to look like a cat.

8 Use self-adhesive photo corners or tape to attach your photos to the pages.

Switchplate cover

This is a fun way to jazz up a light switch!

YOU WILL NEED

- a switchplate cover and screws
- a piece of sandpaper
- a piece of dry spaghetti
- 2 small beads
- a pencil, paints, paintbrushes, white glue, water-based varnish (optional)

1 If you are removing the switchplate cover from the wall, ask an adult to help. Do not lose the screws!

2 Lightly sand the cover. This will help the paint to stick.

3 Draw the cat as shown.

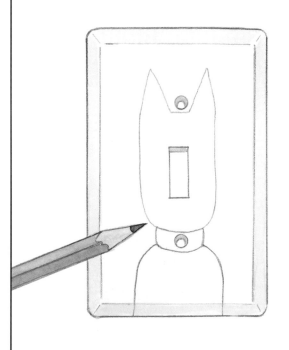

4 Paint the cat and the background. Paint one of the screws the same color as the background. Let the paint dry. Apply a second coat if necessary.

5 Paint the spaghetti black and let it dry.

6 Break the spaghetti into six short pieces and glue them to the cat's face for whiskers. Glue on the beads for eyes.

7 To make the nose, ask an adult to paint the end of the light switch pink.

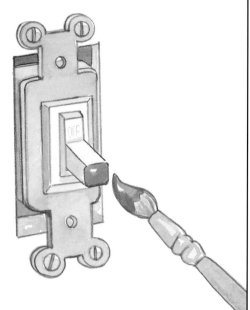

8 If you like, paint the cover and switch with a coat of water-based varnish. When the varnish is dry, ask an adult to reattach the cover.

Accessory organizer

When it comes to organizing hair clips and barrettes, this cat is ready to lend a helping paw.

YOU WILL NEED

- corrugated cardboard, 7 strips each 4 cm x 14 cm (1½ in. x 5½ in.), 1 piece 15 cm x 24 cm (6 in. x 9½ in.), 1 piece 10 cm x 13 cm (4 in. x 5 in.)
- 2 small beads or buttons
- 2 pieces of dry spaghetti
- a ball of yarn
- white glue, a pencil, scissors, paints, paintbrushes, a hammer and 2 small nails

1 Glue three strips of cardboard together. Repeat to make another three-layer strip. Set the pieces aside to dry. These are spacers.

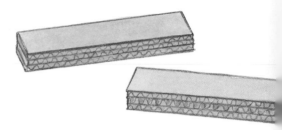

2 On the large piece of cardboard, draw and cut out the shape as shown. This is the cat's body.

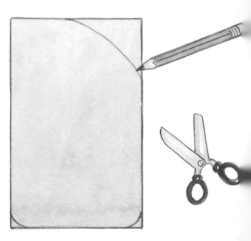

3 Draw the head on the medium-sized cardboard and cut it out.

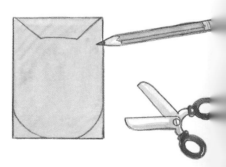

4 On the remaining strip of cardboard, draw the leg shape and cut it out.

5 Glue the head to the front of the body. Let it dry. Glue the leg to the back of the body. Let dry.

6 Draw on details and paint them in. Glue on the beads for eyes. Break the spaghetti into six pieces and glue them on for whiskers.

7 For the tail, cut fifteen 60 cm (24 in.) pieces of yarn. Tie them together with a short piece of yarn, then divide them into three strands and braid them. Tie a short piece of yarn around the end of the braid, then trim it and glue it to the back of the cat.

8 Glue the spacers to the back. They will hold your organizer away from the wall so you can attach clips and slide accessories onto the leg. To attach your organizer to the wall, ask an adult to hammer a nail through each end of the top spacer.

Crazy cat earrings

Make a matching necklace by threading a cord through the loop. Or omit the loop and create a brooch by attaching a pin back.

YOU WILL NEED

- Fimo or other polymer clay in black, white and pink
- 12 wooden toothpicks
- 4 7-mm (5/16-in.) jump rings
- 2 shepherd hooks (ear wires)
- a table knife, scissors, a baking sheet, tin foil, needlenose pliers

1 Use your finger to flatten two marble-sized pieces of black clay into circles about 0.25 cm (1/8 in.) thic

2 Make a small cut in each circle as shown, then spread the circle ou on either side for ears.

3 Roll a pea-sized ball of black clay into a log about 8 cm (3 in.) lon Cut the log in half and form each piec into a loop. Attach a loop to the back each earring.

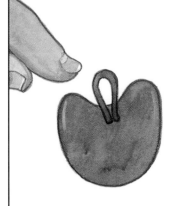

4 To make the mouth and nose, press two pea-sized balls of white clay onto each earring. Cut a pea-sized ball of pink in half and shape each half into a triangle. Press a triangle onto the balls.

6 Cut a 1.5 cm (⅝ in.) piece from the pointy end of each toothpick. Insert three pieces into each white ball for whiskers.

7 With an adult's help, bake the earrings on a foil-lined baking sheet according to the directions on the packages of clay.

8 When the earrings are cool, use the pliers to carefully attach two jump rings and a shepherd hook to each loop.

5 Cut two pea-sized balls of white clay in half. Roll each piece into a ball and flatten it into a circle. Place the circles onto the earrings for eyes. Place a dot of black clay in the center of each.

Puss
pencil case

Another missing pencil?
Detective Kat is on the case.

YOU WILL NEED

- felt, 1 piece 14 cm x 18 cm
(5½ in. x 7 in.),
1 piece 23 cm x 30 cm (9 in. x 12 in.)

- embroidery floss in 2 colors
and a darning needle

- 2 medium-sized buttons

- 3 small craft pom-poms,
2 the same color and 1 black or pink

- 2 small beads

- 6 pieces of black yarn,
each 4 cm (1½ in.) long

- straight pins, scissors, a pen, white glue

1 Make a fold 7.5 cm (3 in.) up
from the bottom of the small piec
of felt and pin it in place.

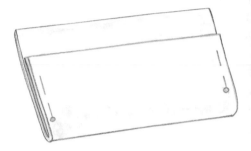

2 Using one color of embroidery
floss and the darning needle,
blanket stitch (see page 5) the sides
together to create a pocket. Remove
the pins.

3 To make the ears, trim the top of
the felt pocket as shown.

4 On the large piece of felt, make a fold 3 cm (5 in.) up from the bottom, then turn the piece over.

Center the pocket along the folded edge, and pin it to the top layer of the large piece of felt.

Unfold the large piece and stitch the inside of the pocket to in several places. Remove the pins.

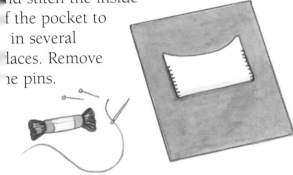

5 Refold the large piece of felt and use the other color of embroidery floss to blanket stitch the sides together.

6 On the flap, make two cuts that are slightly shorter than the buttons. Fold the flap down, and use a pen to mark the center of each of these button holes on the case.

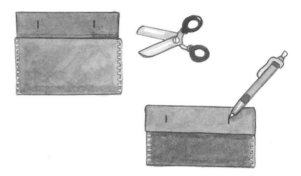

7 Open the flap and sew a button securely to each spot you marked.

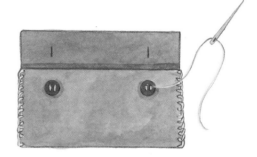

8 Glue the pom-poms to the pocket for a nose and mouth. Glue on the beads for eyes and the pieces of yarn for whiskers.

Catnip container

Turn an ordinary glass jar into a great-looking container for catnip or kitty treats.

YOU WILL NEED

- Fimo or other polymer clay in black, white, pink, green, and yellow
  - a glass jar with a metal lid
- a veiny leaf (a rose leaf works well)
  - a table knife, a needle
  - tin foil, a baking sheet

1 For the head, flatten a Ping-Pong ball-sized piece of black clay into a circle about 0.25 cm (⅛ in.) thick. Make a small cut in the circle as shown, then spread the circle to make ears.

2 Roll two marble-sized balls of white clay and attach them to the head for the mouth. Use the needle to poke three holes in each ball. Flatten a small piece of white clay to make a stripe above the mouth.

3 Form a small piece of pink clay into a triangle-shaped tongue. Place it under the white balls. Press on a pink oval-shaped nose.

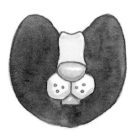

4 Flatten two small white balls and press a dot of black onto each for eyes. Make whiskers and a chin with small rolls of white. Carefully press the cat's head onto the jar.

6 To cover the lid, begin at the outer edge and press the leaves over the edge of the lid. Place the next row of leaves so they overlap the first. Continue, finishing in the center.

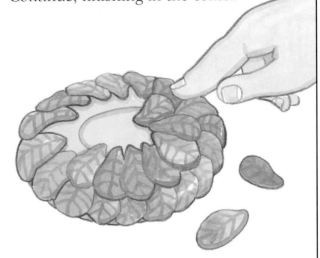

5 Mix small amounts of green and yellow together in balls and flatten into leaf shapes, about 0.25 cm (1/8 in.) thick. Press each one onto the veiny side of a leaf. Peel off the clay leaf and press it onto the jar. Cover the bottom half of the jar with overlapping leaves.

7 With an adult's help, bake the lid and jar on a tin foil-lined baking sheet according to the directions on the packages of clay. Let them cool completely. If a leaf falls off after baking, reattach it with two-part epoxy or an adhesive made to glue plastic.

Dough picture frame

With a bit of flour and salt, you can cook up this PURRRfect gift for a cat lover.

YOU WILL NEED

- 375 mL (1½ c.) all-purpose flour
- 175 mL (¾ c.) salt
- 150 mL (⅔ c.) lukewarm water
- 10 mL (2 tsp.) cooking oil
- 7 wooden toothpicks
- a piece of construction paper 13 cm x 13 cm (5 in. x 5 in.)
- a piece of yarn 15 cm (6 in.) long
- a mixing bowl and spoon, plastic wrap, wax paper, a rolling pin, a baking sheet, a table knife, a drinking straw, paints, paintbrushes, acrylic varnish, white glue

1 Use the spoon to mix the flour, salt, water and oil in the bowl. With your hands, knead the dough for 10 minutes. Cover with plastic wrap and let sit for 30 minutes.

2 On a piece of wax paper, roll out about two-thirds of the dough into a circle 23 cm (9 in.) across and 0.5 cm (¼ in.) thick. Set the wax paper and the circle on the baking sheet.

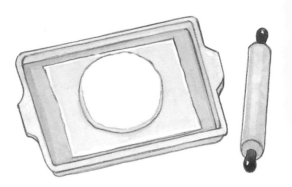

3 Mix a small ball of dough with a few drops of water to make a paste. Cut a 9 cm (3½ in.) circle from the center of the large circle. Use the paste to attach the small circle as shown.

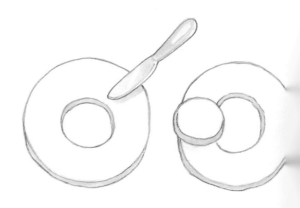

4 Follow the steps below to paste each piece to the circle to make the rest of the cat. Use toothpicks for whiskers.

5 For the mouse, make a pear shape and attach it to the top of the frame. Roll a tail, and flatten two balls into ear shapes. Make small balls for a nose and eyes. Use the remaining toothpicks for whiskers.

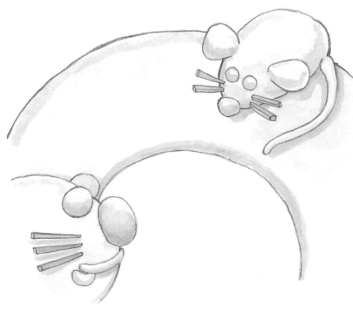

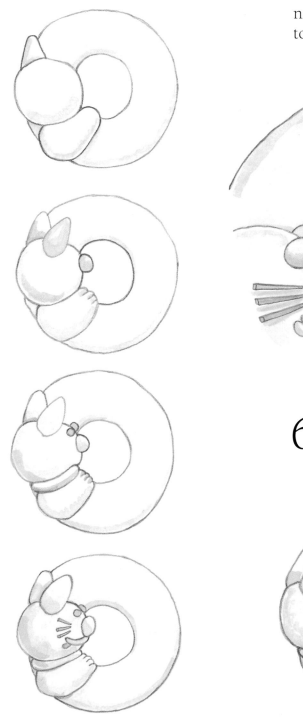

6 Decorate the rest of the frame with small balls of dough.

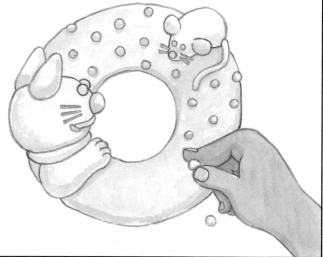

Instructions continue on the next page ☞

7 Use the straw to poke two holes near the top of the frame.

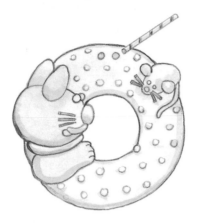

8 Ask an adult to place the baking sheet on the middle rack of a 120°C (250°F) oven for about 5 hours. When the frame is hard and just golden, turn off the heat and let the frame cool in the oven.

9 Paint the frame. After 24 hours, apply a coat of acrylic varnish to the front and back.

10 To make a photo pocket, run a line of glue along three sides of the construction paper and glue it to the back of the frame with the opening at the top.

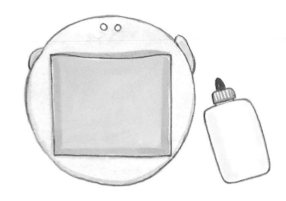

11 Thread the yarn through the holes in the frame and tie a double knot to create a loop. Hang your frame in a dry place because it may go soft in a damp basement or bathroom.

Alley-cat bookend

To make a set of bookends, double the amount of materials you will need.

YOU WILL NEED

- corrugated cardboard,
1 piece 15 cm x 25 cm (6 in. x 10 in.),
5 pieces each 2.5 cm x 15 cm
(1 in. x 6 in.),
1 piece the same size as
the bottom of the can
- a clean tin can, about 398 mL (14 oz.)
- 250 mL (1 c.) sand or small pebbles
- a small plastic bag and twist tie
- 250 mL (1 c.) self-hardening
modeling clay
- several short pieces of wire
or toothpicks
- a pencil, a ruler, a utility knife or
scissors, paints, paintbrushes, white glue,
masking tape, paper, a table knife

1 Mark a point on the center of each long side of the large piece of cardboard and lay the ruler across so the edge is touching both points. Score the cardboard with the utility knife by making a light cut along the ruler. Do not cut completely through.

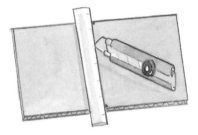

2 Turn the cardboard over and paint one half green and the other half blue.

3 To make the fence, cut one end of each strip of cardboard into a point. Paint the pieces, then glue them to the blue half of the cardboard.

Instructions continue on the next page ☞

4 Run a line of glue around the bottom and along the side seam of the can. Center the can along the edge of the green half of cardboard. Fold the fence against the glue and hold it in place with a piece of tape until it is dry.

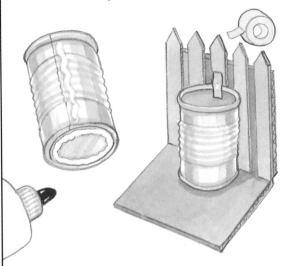

6 For the lid, paint the circle of cardboard gray. Fold a small strip of paper and glue it to the circle for a handle. Fill the garbage can with bits of paper crumpled to look like garbage.

5 Glue some sand around the garbage can, then pour the rest in the plastic bag and tie it with the twist tie. Trim the top of the bag if necessary and set it in the can.

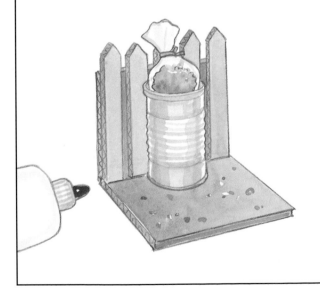

7 To make the cat, roll a small sausage-sized cylinder of clay for the body. Roll four baby finger-sized cylinders for legs. Roll a small cylinder for a tail. Press the legs and tail onto the body. Wet your finger and smooth them out where they join.

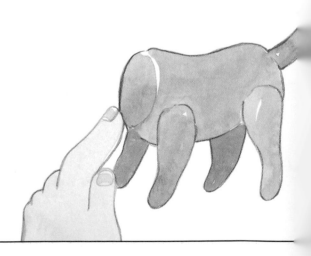

8 Roll a ball of clay for the head. Pinch part of the ball into two small triangle-shaped ears. Press a marble-sized ball of clay onto the head, then use the knife to cut a mouth. Press balls of clay on for a nose and eyes.

10 Make small cuts for toes, and use wire or toothpicks for whiskers.

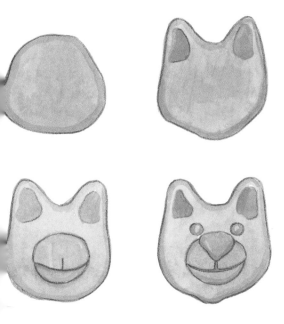

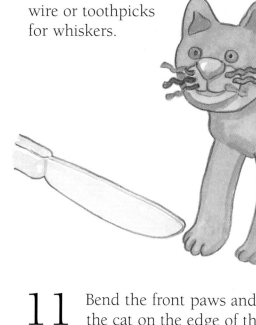

11 Bend the front paws and hang the cat on the edge of the can. Shape the back legs into a pose that you like, then set the cat aside to dry completely (this could take several days). Paint the cat when it is dry and then put it back on the can.

9 Press the head in place. Wet your finger and smooth out the join.

Decorated lampshade

If your lampshade is smaller or larger, adjust the number and position of the cats to fit, or try making your own designs!

YOU WILL NEED

- a white cloth-covered hardback lampshade, about 30 cm (12 in.) across the bottom and 20 cm (8 in.) high
- black dimensional fabric paint
- a black marker and tracing paper, scissors, masking tape, a pencil, paints, paintbrushes

1 Photocopy — or use the marker and tracing paper to trace — three copies of each pattern on page 40. Cut out the patterns.

2 Tape one pattern (drawing side facing out) to the inside of the lampshade, close to the side seam and along the bottom edge.

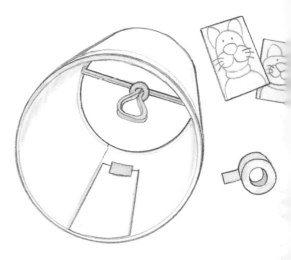

3 Tape the second pattern about 8 cm (3 in.) from the first. Continue taping the patterns to the inside of the lampshade, alternating the patterns and spacing them evenly.

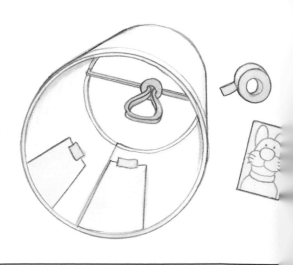

4 Check your design. If you can't see the patterns clearly, hold the shade up to a light. When you are happy with the design, trace the patterns onto the lampshade with the pencil. Remove the patterns.

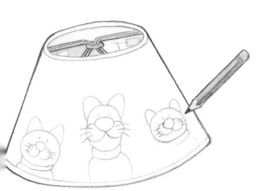

5 Carefully paint the cats and let them dry.

6 Outline the cats with the dimensional fabric paint. (To avoid splatters, occasionally tap the nozzle of the tube on your work surface to remove air bubbles.) Do only one or two cats at a time and let them dry so you don't smudge them.

7 Carefully draw a line of fabric paint along the top and bottom edges of the lampshade. Let the paint dry.

OTHER IDEAS

Make holes along the bottom edge of the shade with a hole punch. Tie a string of beads or pom-poms to each hole.

Lampshade patterns (for page 38)

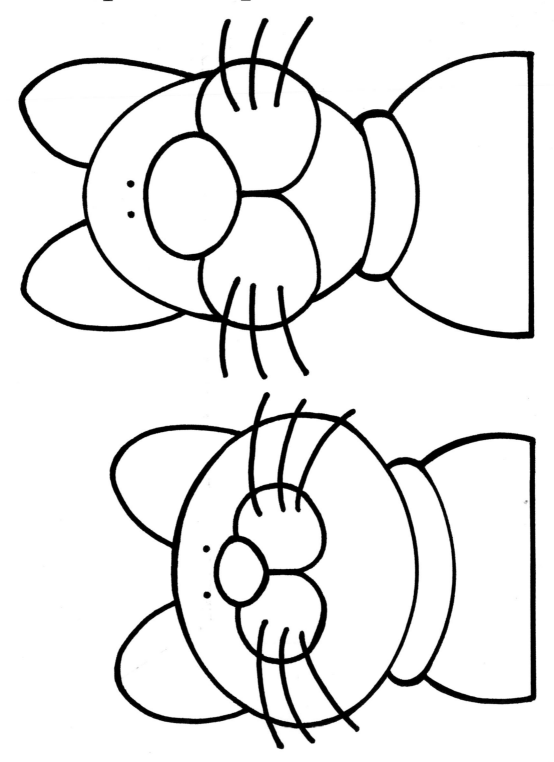